Cars

by Julie Murray

ABDO
TRANSPORTATION
Kids

Visit us at www.abdopublishing.com

Published by Abdo Kids, a division of ABDO, PO Box 398166, Minneapolis, Minnesota 55439.

Copyright © 2015 by Abdo Consulting Group, Inc. International copyrights reserved in all countries. No part of this book may be reproduced in any form without written permission from the publisher.

Printed in the United States of America, North Mankato, Minnesota.

032014

092014

 PRINTED ON RECYCLED PAPER

Photo Credits: Glow Images, iStock, Shutterstock, Thinkstock

Production Contributors: Teddy Borth, Jennie Forsberg, Grace Hansen

Design Contributors: Dorothy Toth, Laura Rask

Library of Congress Control Number: 2013953008

Cataloging-in-Publication Data

Murray, Julie.

 Cars / Julie Murray.

  p. cm. -- (Transportation)

ISBN 978-1-62970-079-3 (lib. bdg.)

Includes bibliographical references and index.

1. Automobiles--Juvenile literature.   I. Title.

629.22--dc23

2013953008

Table of Contents

Cars 4

Parts of a Car 6

Different Kinds of Cars 12

More Facts 22

Glossary 23

Index 24

Abdo Kids Code. 24

Cars

Many people ride in cars every day. Cars get people from one place to another.

4

5

Parts of a Car

Cars have a body and four wheels. The steering wheel turns the wheels.

The engine powers the car.

The seats and controls are

inside the car.

9

The seat belts and air bags keep you safe. The headlights help the driver see at night.

Different Kinds of Cars

Most cars need **fuel** to run.

They run on gas or **diesel**.

Some cars are **electric**.

They run on a battery that

is charged by electricity.

LADEN... 92%
CHARGING...

15

Some cars are called **hybrids**.

They often run on gas or

diesel and a battery.

Smart cars are often used in the city. They are small and easy to park.

19

Police cars have special lights and **sirens**. These help others know the police car is coming.

More Facts

- The first cars were steam powered. Today, most cars are powered by gasoline.

- Cars are one of the most recycled items in the world.

- The first paper speeding ticket was issued in 1904 in Ohio. The man ticketed was driving 12 miles per hour (19 km/h).

- A car is also called an automobile. That is a French word.

Glossary

diesel – a type of fuel for diesel engines.

electric – using electricity.

fuel – an energy source for engines.

hybrid – combining two or more ways of operation. Hybrid cars use gas and electricity.

siren – a loud noise used as a warning device.

Index

air bags 10

battery 14, 16

body 6

controls 8

diesel 12, 16

electric 14

engine 8

fuel 12

gas 12, 16

headlights 10

hybrid 16

police car 20

seat belt 10

seats 8

siren 20

smart car 18

steering wheel 6

wheels 6

abdokids.com

Use this code to log on to abdokids.com and access crafts, games, videos and more!

Abdo Kids Code:
TCK0793